ABOUT PRAYER!

- A Beginner's Guide -

Don Wilkerson

Contents

INTRODUCTION
THE KINDERGARTEN OF PRAYER

L et's be honest! We believe more in the importance of prayer than in the actual practice of prayer. You would be surprised as to who are the prayer-less ones in the body of Christ. Prayer, for some people, is like dieting. Many would like to lose weight, but never do what's necessary to lose those extra pounds. Are you one who knows you should pray more—even daily—but rarely get around to it? When you do pray, is it like a 911 emergency call prayer? Like the sailor at sea when he thought the ship was going to capsize, he got on his knees and cried out, "Lord, you know I have not bothered You for years. And if You save us now, I won't bother You again for years."

Prayer is seen as hard work, not because it is, but because we treat it as such. Praying is like exercising or running. Deciding to make a habit of it is not usually a priority, but it should be. We keep hearing sermons on the importance of prayer. No doubt, you've heard of numerous answers to prayer and had some yourself. And yet, have you made it a regular practice?

But you are those who forsake the Lord, who forget My Holy Mountain (Isaiah 65:11).

The mountain here can refer to the mountain of prayer. Why is prayer near the bottom of a Christian's practice? Given the choice of paying ten percent of one's income as a tithe to God and the church and giving God ten minutes of our day to prayer, tithing appears to be the easier way to go. Pay or pray? How about pay and pray!

We neglect prayer because it seems so hard, but it really isn't. Just listen to a child's prayer and you'll realize, even if you're in the kindergarten stage of prayer yourself, it's a simple act of obedience that we should do on a regular basis.

If by now you are feeling convicted about your prayerlessness, you might set this book aside. Or, out of curiosity or conviction, you realize that daily prayer is at least as important as daily hygiene and brushing your teeth. It's just as important as breathing. So please, take a deep breath and continue.

Another title of this book might be *Prayer for Dummies.* Don't take this as an insult. I consider myself a "dummy," too, for whenever I have preached, taught, or written about prayer, it's almost always directed to the choir—those who already pray. Yet, I realize now a good number of people I minister to do not pray regularly. I fear to know the actual number. This has motivated me to share this *Beginner's Guide* to prayer. I hope that reading this will result in a new beginning in your daily prayer life.

I'm writing to both the non-prayers and the prayer relapsers. I know that deep inside, all of us who are followers of Christ believe in the importance of prayer. Most books written on prayer are to those who do pray, but it is one of those practices often neglected for various reasons. So, we buy books on prayer out of guilt in the hopes of stirring ourselves to become consistent in prayer.

Prayer for the prayer-less believer is like knowing you ought to eat better food, but still, you take the fork in hand, bite into that chocolate cake, committing not the unpardonable sin, but the sin you keep pardoning yourself for, and your health and weight gets worse. Pardon the scriptural pun: "Let us lay aside every weight, and the sin that does so easily beset us, and let us run with patience the race set before us" (Hebrews 12:1).

"Let us run...."

Run to God! Run to the prayer closet. Let's run to the altar and confess our prayerlessness.

Prayer is necessary to run the race of serving God. It cannot be delegated. I had a brother who once joked, "I think I'll pay someone to run for me." We do enlist others to pray for us in times of great need, but prayer is most effective when we "ask, seek, and knock" ourselves at heaven's door.

My goal in writing this is to challenge you to run to God—to go before Him, talk to Him, and develop a consistent daily time of prayer with Him. If you are a newborn Christian starting your new life as a pray-er, it can become a practice done naturally and supernaturally. A.W. Tozer wrote,

In my mind, the most important discipline in my life has to do with my prayer life. It is one thing to talk about prayer. No matter where you go, Christians celebrate the virtue of prayer and a prayer life. Yes, I find it rather strange, when you get down to the practical aspects, very few Christians really engage in the discipline of prayer to the extent that it is available to them in their Christian experience.[1]

One more thing, before we begin this journey *About Prayer,* is to keep in mind that the first and most important prayer is the sinner's prayer. Anyone who sincerely seeks mercy from God shall have it. Whatever your previous condition — a sinner in general biblical terms or deeply mired in the pit of sin — if you come to Jesus, the Mediator between us and God, you will be saved immediately and forever.

The prayer of the saved person is a bit different because it's based on a relationship, like that of a child to a parent. Charles Spurgeon, the great preacher in the 1800's in London, gives the following illustration of the prayer of the saved sinner:

> If a hungry person were at your door asking for bread, you'd give it to him, whatever might be his character. You would also give your child food, whatever may be his behavior. You will not deny your child anything that is

necessary for life, but there are many other things your child may desire that you will give if he is obedient but will withhold if he is rebellious. This illustrates how far the parental government of God will push this matter [of prayer] and where it will go. Understand also that this refers not so much to God's hearing the prayer of His servants now and then, for that He will do even when His servants are out of course with Him and He is hiding His face from them. The power in prayer here intended is continuous and absolute so that "Whatever we ask, we receive from Him."[2]

In other words, prayer for the sinner who is seeking salvation is not based on the goodness of the one who prays but on the goodness of God to save all who come to Him. Yet, for those who are servants of the Lord, prayers are answered in accordance with our faith and the closeness of our walk with God. The Bible says, *"If I regard in iniquity in my heart, the Lord will not hear"* (Psalm 66:18). Psalm 66, verses 16 to 20 in the Message Bible reads,

> All believers, come here and listen, let me tell you what God did for me. I called out to him with my mouth, my tongue shaped the sounds of music. If I had been cozy with evil, the Lord would have never listened. But he most assuredly did listen.

He came on the double when he heard my prayer. Blessed be God: he didn't turn a deaf ear. He stayed with me, loyal in his love.

Note: Singing to the Lord is a vital ingredient to a vibrant prayer life. I have added at the end of some of the Chapters lyrics to various songs and hymns.

Song 1
I Can Pray

You say I'm not able
I'm too young or I'm too old
And I can't sing or teach
And no title do I hold
Lord, what can I do?
For I want to do my part
And I want to help the hurting
With all my heart

I can pray till the walls come down
Until there is healing all around
That's something I can do
I can pray in my secret place
Calling on Your Name
That's something I can do
I can pray

My family shows no interest
My child has gone so far
Thou I try my best to reach them
Their heart just seems so hard
Lord, what can I do?
To help bring them back to You
For my family's lost and dying
And my words don't get through

ABOUT PRAYER!

You may not be a Sunday school teacher
You may not be able to sing
But friend there's something we all can do
You can pray
In your secret place
Calling on His name
That's something you can do

You can pray, I can pray, we can pray
I can pray, you can pray
I know you hear us Lord when we pray
We will pray
I can pray
Will you pray?[3]

1

ABBA FATHER

**Pray like this: Our Father in heaven,
may your name be kept holy.**
(Matthew 6:9 NLT)

In writing about prayer and why we don't pray more regularly, I have discovered to my surprise one of the reasons has to do with what I call father issues. By this I mean two specific issues: one is regarding relationships with biological fathers, and the other is our relationship with our heavenly Father and how one affects the other. With believers, these two fathers are intertwined. In other words, the relationship with earthly fathers can be projected onto how we view God the Father. This, in turn, can affect our prayer life.

One young lady told me, "I love Jesus. I love God! But when it comes to praying, 'Our Father in heaven,' I have a hard time with that." She knew this was because her earthly father abandoned the family when she was eleven years old, and he's not been in her life since.

A woman from England who did an internship in the ministry I directed told me how she discovered later in life that on her birth certificate her father was not her biological father, and she shut him out of her life from that time on. He passed away and she did not attend his funeral. She confessed how guilty she felt for not even attending. She said, "Every time the name father is mentioned, I associate it with my earthly father."

My friend, author Charles Simpson, writing in his excellent book *The Bosom of the Father*, states:

> Tragically, many people have suffered abuse and neglect from a father figure. Martin Luther is quoted as saying, "My father once whipped me so hard I ran away. I hated him...." Is it any wonder that he also wrote: "From early childhood, I was accustomed to turn pale and tremble whenever I heard the name of Christ mentioned, for I was taught to look upon Him as a stern and wrathful judge."[4]

On the other hand, positive lessons can be learned in the relationship between an earthly father and Father God. The most important one is the Father Son connection as revealed in Scripture. In John, Chapters 15 to 17, Jesus mentions His Father some 22 times. In Chapter 17, this mention is in the form of a prayer. At times, Jesus the Son addresses His Father as "My Father," and other times, He addresses Him as "You."

Jesus models prayer as time spent between a father and a son, or, in this case, between the Son of God and His heavenly Father.

It should be noted in His teaching on prayer, Jesus said,

But you, when you pray, go into your room, and when you have shut your door, pray to Your Father who is in secret (Matthew 6:6).

This is not just about shutting the door to outside distractions that are hindrances to prayer, but it's also about an intimacy between the Son and the Father, between the child of God and Father God. Public and corporate prayers are good and necessary but there is something very special between a father and his child being with each other.

This lack of understanding of the intimacy of prayer, I am convinced, is one of the reasons we do not view it as the highest, holiest shut-in-together with Father God in the secret place that it should be. Any young child or adult who experiences quality time with an earthly father is emotionally, psychologically, and spiritually healthier. As in the natural, so in the supernatural kingdom of God. The secret place of prayer with our loving Father lifts prayer into a much higher place. Is this what is missing in our teaching, understanding, and practice of prayer? It turns prayer into an audience with the Father, and not just the One to Whom requests are made. It is much more than that because such requests are based on a loving relationship.

Dr. F.W. Krummacher, a fiery German preacher in the 1800's shared the following thoughts:

When you stand before His gate, knock loudly and boldly. Do not knock as a beggar knocks, but as one who belongs in the house. Not as a vagabond, who is afraid of the police, but as a friend and an intimate acquaintance. Not as one who is apprehensive of being troublesome or of coming at an improper time, but as a guest who may be assured of a hearty welcome.[5]

It would be a shame to accuse *"Our Father in heaven"* of being like a bad earthly father. He is in no way such a Father. If you had or have a father issue, focus your faith on God, the perfect Father.

I do understand how we might not identify with God as "Our Father." Even Jesus, in His teaching on prayer, used the example of an evil father who, despite not being a good and righteous father, can at the same time and on occasion, give good gifts to his children. But our perfect Father does not give out gifts sparingly, nor does He demand we earn those gifts. He's not tight-fisted. *"How much more will your heavenly Father give the Holy Spirit to those who ask Him"* (Luke 11:13). The contrast made in these verses between an earthly father and our heavenly Father refers to the type of giving. Yes, thank God if you've had a giving earthly father. But *the* Father is *"much more"* than simply a giver. Why would you want to put Father God in the same category as your earthly father even if your own father always deserved the Father-of-the-Year Award?

Paul the Apostle understood prayer as approaching an Abba Father, for he wrote in Galatians 4:6:

> And because you are sons, God sent forth the Spirit of His Son into your hearts crying, "Abba Father."

The point Paul is making, I believe, is that when we allow the Holy Spirit to pray through us, it is an Abba Father prayer; a prayer of God's child to the One who is a listening, loving, and caring Father.

Earthly fathers can be distant and, at times, seem unapproachable. But Abba means "my father." Jesus makes this real in His prayer recorded in John 17 when He prayed, *"You, Father, are in Me, and I in You."* This oneness that exists between Son and Father raises prayer to its highest level.

Paul also mentions Abba Father in Romans 8:15 saying,

> You received the Spirit of adoption by whom we cry out, "Abba Father."

The context of this is that because of our sin nature we must be born again. We are not God's son or daughter by natural birth but by a supernatural rebirth. Then He adopts us, and when He does, He becomes our "Abba Father," and then we can joyfully claim Him as "My Father." So begins the prayer Jesus taught His disciples.

As introduced earlier, it is strange that in today's culture, one of the reasons we don't pray more is that many have a father issue when it comes to our biological fathers.

Here are a few earthly father issues that may be the reason we do not talk to God our heavenly Father more:

1. Earthly fathers sometimes neglect us.

A main reason why unbelieving people do not embrace God the Father is because, for them, God is not a factor in their life. For example, on occasion, when having a special need or problem, they may have tried praying a sort of 911 prayer, but the answer didn't come when or as they expected. How strange it is not to want God to intrude in your life, and then suddenly you need Him, and you're surprised, even angry, that He didn't answer the way you thought He should have.

At a time of future judgment when we all must give an account before God the Father, He will put His judgment robe on and ask us a reason why He should not pronounce us "guilty" and sentence us to eternal separation from Him. Unfortunately, on that day, God may say, "You wanted life on your own terms and your way, so I grant you your desire." In other words, God will say, "Have it your way."

This is the father issue of those who never knew the Father. What about those who believe? *"The eyes of the Lord are on the righteous and his ears open to their prayers"* (1 Peter 3:12).

2. Fathers often seem remote to their kids.

Even when an earthly father might be a good financial provider and thus is considered a good father, they may not realize their children need emotional support and father time from babyhood, through childhood, and even into adulthood. Time spent between son (or daughter) and father at any age is crucial. When that is missing, this too can be a father issue carried over into our spiritual lives, making us feel like Father God is distant, as well. I think when God our Father in heaven sees His children comparing Him to their earthly fathers, He desires to remind us, "I'm not that way." The Psalmist wrote: *"He will say to me, 'You are my Father and my God, as well the mighty rock where I am safe'"* (CEV).

3. Some Fathers are abusive.

An abusive father is not only hurting the ones they should be protecting, but they are also damaging their children's ability to see and know the goodness of God the Father, a double and horrible offense.

There are some comparisons between a good father and *"Our Father in heaven,"* the One who will be there whenever you need Him. Like the father in the Parable of the Prodigal Son, our heavenly Father is a runner:

And he arose and came to his father. But way off, when he was still a great way off, his father had compassion and ran and fell on his neck and kissed him" (Luke 15:20).

Another way to interpret this is whenever it states the father of the prodigal son saw him and ran towards him, it is an analogy of our Father in heaven. We were estranged from our Lord and Savior and our Father in heaven, so when the Scripture says, *"When he was a great way off"* we can see ourselves as that prodigal, distanced from our Father God who runs to us, accepts our confession of our sin, and wholeheartedly welcomes us back.

Song 2

This Is My Father's World

This is my Father's world
And to my listening ears
All nature sings, and round me rings
The music of the spheres

This is my Father's world
I rest me in the thought
Of rocks and trees, of skies and seas—
His hand the wonders wrought

This is my Father's world
The birds their carols raise
The morning light, the lily white
Declare their Maker's praise

This is my Father's world
He shines in all that's fair
In the rustling grass I hear Him pass
He speaks to me everywhere

This is my Father's world
O let me ne'er forget
That though the wrong seems oft so strong
God is the Ruler yet

ABOUT PRAYER!

This is my Father's world
Why should my heart be sad?
The Lord is King: let the heavens ring
God reigns; let earth be glad[6]

2

CAN YOU STILL GO TO HEAVEN IF YOU DON'T PRAY?

Let us therefore come boldly to the throne of grace, that we may obtain mercy and find grace to help in time of need.
(Hebrews 4:16)

Let me put prayer in the context of the question: Will we go to heaven based on whether we have a prayer life or not? Is our heaven and our eternal destiny at stake if we do not pray regularly? Is prayer a command, an invitation, or an option?

The answer is no, and yes? How so? We must ask to be saved. That asking comes in the form of prayer, often called "the sinner's prayer." Romans 10:9 says,

> If you confess with the mouth the Lord Jesus and believe in your heart that God raised Him from the dead, you will be saved.

A few verses later (10:13), the same is repeated in these words: *"For whosoever shall call upon the Lord shall be saved."* Initially, then, God requires us to ask in prayer to be saved. God does nothing against your will. Our Father wants to be wanted. He knocks at our door, but we must invite Him to come into our life.

My wife, Cindy, and I like to watch Hallmark movies from time to time (and now the faith and family channel called the Great American Family Network). The movies are often about a couple connecting or reconnecting after having dated in high school or some time before. As the story develops, there comes a time when the reconnection does not seem to be working. Then one or the other says, "We need to talk." The talk refers to coming to an understanding of where they stand in their reconnection and what one or the other thinks about what the future holds for them.

Is the Holy Spirit saying to you, "We need to talk."? It is a message that can apply not just to natural relationships, but to a supernatural relationship with God our Father and His Son Jesus. Might the Spirit be saying to you, "We need to talk."? Prayer is talking on the most fundamental level. Perhaps believers do not pray more because when they hear a pastoral prayer in church with its intensity, high volume, and perfect choice of words, it seems, well, too heavenly for them. But I don't think God ever intended prayer to be just liturgical, ritualistic, or belonging exclusively to the priesthood or the official ministers.

I personally think a pastoral prayer should be passionate, articulate, and Scriptural. Being seasoned in the school of prayer, I know the difference between church prayers and private prayers. A.W. Tozer, in *Delighting in God*, wrote:

> Sometimes in our prayers, we get rather eloquent. I have discovered that when I am eloquent in my prayers, I am not getting much accomplished. My eloquence sometimes gets in the way of really connecting with God.[7]

Those new to the faith and church life may hear for the first time a pastoral prayer and think they will never be able to pray like that! Before you qualify for a PhD in prayer (if there is such a thing), first you must enter the School of Kindergarten Prayer and learn the basics of praying.

When the disciples asked Jesus who He considered the greatest in His kingdom, He did not say, "Those who pray the best and the longest." Rather,

> He called a little child to Him, set him in the midst, and said, "Assuredly I say to you, unless you be converted and become little children, you will by no means enter the kingdom of God" (Matthew 18:1-3).

I used to listen to a well-known revival preacher who would criticize the hymn that said, *"Just a little talk with Jesus makes it right."* (The lyrics are pasted at the end of this Chapter.) He would say the problem in the church today is there is *just a little talk with Jesus* going on. I would not differ with him. However, *a little talk* is better than no talk at all, that is, no prayer at all.

The prayer that is essential to get us to heaven is, as I have stated, the sinner's prayer. With this prayer, we enter into a relationship with the Father and His Son. In prayer, we get a taste of heaven on our way to heaven. Frankly, I have never had anyone ask me, "If I don't pray, will I go to heaven?" I invented the question myself and did so to highlight that prayer should *"...not be of works lest anyone should boast"* (Ephesians 2:9). I wonder why would a believer who knows they are going to heaven (and that prayer is a taste of heaven) not make prayer an on-going practice and part of their life as a Christian?

The assurance of heaven and eternal life enables the believer to *"come boldly to the throne of grace"* (Hebrews 4:16). We have an open link to heaven through our relationship with the Father, Son, and Holy Ghost who are attuned to hear the faintest cry of the feeblest child of God.

Heaven begins the moment we ask Christ into our heart and life. A line from an old song says, *"Heaven came down, and glory filled my soul."*[8] It is a shame that we are often taught that prayer is primarily a duty and not a delight.

Salvation is by faith and prayer is done voluntarily by faith. The Bible says,

> For by grace are you have been saved through faith, and that not of yourselves;

it is the gift of God, not of works, lest anyone should boast (Ephesians 2:8).

In some church traditions, Christian practices are viewed as "works" — such as giving to the church and the poor, loving your neighbor, etc. — works that gain brownie points with God. The practice of prayer is also placed in that same category of "works."

Certainly, God is pleased when we pray, but besides the prayer unto salvation, our prayers do not qualify us for the eternal reward of going to heaven. Prayer does help us on our way there.

A German proverb states: *"Pray as though no work will help and work as though no prayer will help."*[9] When as a teenager I began developing a personal prayer time, I often saw it as a "work." I had the thought, "Lord, doesn't my time spent in prayer merit something?" as if God owed me something in return.

We've answered the question that prayer alone does not "get us to heaven," but it does give us a taste of it. Knowing this, why would we not want to pray? Prayer, like kindergarten, should be about the joy of knowing and being alive in Christ. To the kindergartener, school is about the joy of learning and discovery. It's about increasing in knowledge. It is the same with prayer. We gain the knowledge of who God is and what He wants to do in our lives. Prayer is like entering a door of which behind it are things never known or seen before. The more we pray, the more doors open to the vastness of what God has prepared for His people. 1 Corinthians 2: 9 says:

ABOUT PRAYER!

No one has ever seen or heard anything like this, never so much as imagined anything quite like it—what God has arranged for those who love Him (NLT).

What an invitation this above verse is for prayer! Prayer at its best is the beginning of knowing God. It opens to us the treasure of knowing who God is and who we are in relation to Him. If it initially takes viewing prayer as a duty, then so be it. But it is so much more than that. Prayer is a relationship, like talking to a best friend. It is the talk of two in love. Yes, we grow more mature in prayer when we graduate from kindergarten, but we miss something when we do not see prayer at its most basic level—two beings spending time together, talking, being in each other's presence. I used to wonder as a youngster when during the evening, I'd be playing with some toy, Dad would be reading a magazine and Mother would be knitting. They rarely exchanged words. They didn't need to. They were enjoying the presence of one another. Someone has said, "Prayer is wonderful, and sometimes it employs words."

Prayer's most basic role is talking to God. Beyond that, it is enjoying the silence and sensing His presence in our lives. You can get to heaven without a prayer life, but if you want to enjoy God's presence at a higher level now, then spend time with Him, either with words or without words. I have always been overwhelmed when reading John in Revelation writing of a time when *"There was silence in heaven about half an hour"* (Revelation 8:1). This is written in light of the fact that four verses later, it says, *"There were noises, thunders, lightening and an earthquake."* Imagine such silence preceding such ear-splitting sounds. In prayer, it's possible to be so overwhelmed by God's power, goodness, love, mercy, and grace that it leaves us speechless. I am experiencing more and more of this in my elder years.

> Then are they glad because they are quiet;
> so He guides them to their desired haven
> (Psalm 107:3).

No one need ever be lonely again when they learn to be, as an old gospel song says, shut in with God.

> Shut in with God in a secret place
> There by the Spirit behold His face
> Gaining more power to run in the race
> Oh, I love to be shut in with God.[10]

Song 3
Just A Little Talk With Jesus

I once was lost in sin
but Jesus took me in
And then a little light from heaven filled my soul
It bathed my heart in love
and it wrote my name above
And just a little talk with my Jesus
made me whole.

Have a little talk with Jesus
Tell him all about our troubles
Hear our fainted cry, answer by and by
Feel a little prayer wheel turning
Know a little fire is burning
Find a little talk with Jesus makes it right.

Sometimes my path grows dreary
Without a ray of cheer
And then a cloud of doubt may hide the day
The mists of sin may rise
And hide the starry skies
But just a little talk with Jesus clears the way.

Have a little talk with Jesus
Tell him all about our troubles
Hear our fainted cry, answer by and by
Feel a little prayer wheel turning
Know a little fire is burning
Find a little talk with Jesus makes it right.

JUST A LITTLE TALK WITH JESUS

I may have doubts and fears
My eyes be filled with tears
But Jesus is a friend who watches day and night
I go to him in prayer
He knows my every care
And just a little talk with my Jesus makes it right.

Have a little talk with Jesus
Tell him all about our troubles
Hear our fainted cry, answer by and by
Feel a little prayer wheel turning
Know a little fire is burning
Find a little talk with Jesus makes it right

Find a little talk with Jesus makes it right[11]

3

PRAYER: DUTY OR DELIGHT?

For the Lord your God is living among you.
He is a mighty savior.
He will take delight in you with gladness.
With His love, He will calm all your fears.
He will rejoice over you with joyful songs.
(Zephaniah 3:17 NLT)

Prayer is not one of the Ten Commandments. While answering the disciple's questions about prayer, Jesus did not mention prayer as a commandment. Instead, He said, *"When you pray…"* All throughout Scripture it is assumed that God's followers will engage in the spiritual practice of prayer. Jesus also said, *"Men ought always to pray, and not lose heart"* (Luke 18:1). In other places, the Scriptures speak of prayer as a command, even if not so defined.

Prayer as a practice is a duty that is simply assumed throughout Scripture. The first reference to prayer in the Bible is after Seth, the son of Noah, gave birth to a son named Enoch. Genesis 4:26 says, *"Then men began to call on the name of the Lord."* Enoch was a preview of the Rapture of the Church in that he walked with God and the Lord took him up to heaven, not through death, but by a supernatural translation. Seth learned something about God and prayer from his father Enoch.

The next scriptural reference to prayer is when Noah exited the ark and *"built an altar to the Lord"* (Genesis 8:20). When the Lord appeared to Abram, promising him the land of Canaan, his response was that *"he built an altar to the Lord who had appeared to him"* (Genesis 12:7). There are also references of Isaac, Joshua, Gideon, and others building altars to the Lord. When the Tabernacle was built in the wilderness, the command was to also build there an altar. It was for sacrifice, a picture of the future death of the Lamb of God for our sins. The altars of sacrifice became meeting places with God. Prayer became the normal response to God's appearances and His promises to our godly forefathers.

It is clear that the regular practice of believers throughout the ages has been to engage in prayer as their spiritual duty. It's when God's people turn away from the altar of God that they have to be called back again and again to the meeting place with Him. And the neglect of prayer became a sign of disobedience to the Lord. Obedience is a command and thereby, of necessity, prayer is viewed as a command. It was not so from the beginning. Prayer, much like hunger and thirst, is simply a response to our spiritual needs in the same way hunger and thirst is to our physical needs. We don't need to be commanded to come to the dinner table, but we are commanded to regularly observe the Lord's Table through Communion.

Should we pray because we have an obligation, a duty to pray? Yes!

In the natural realm, as law-abiding citizens, we have a duty to pay taxes, enforced by the laws of the land. Prayer, on the other hand, is a voluntary practice that we "ought" always to do. Perhaps this is why some of us do not pray.

If pray is done merely as a duty, is it less effective? Not as all. If it takes a sense of duty to pray, so be it. But didn't the Bible, even Jesus, condemn the religious zealots of His day for their ritualistic prayers? Jesus was referring to a type of prayer, not making a statement as if prayer was not to be a part of our Christian walk. Psalm 32:6 says,

> For this cause everyone who is godly shall pray to You in a time when you may be found.

When can God be found? At any time and all times. A.W. Tozer wrote,

> Not to pray when we should pray is like failing to open a letter full of good news.[12]

I grew up in a household with a daily family altar, a specific time and place for prayer. We children never saw it as a duty, just a normal part of being Christians. Sometimes when we had our Wilkerson family prayer time, the whole neighborhood knew about it. My brother Jerry would come outside and holler, "Don, Ruth, David—it's time to pray." This household routine was as sacred as if it were a church service. I don't ever recall complaints from any of my siblings questioning why we had to gather as a family for prayer. It was a normal and accepted duty.

So, it ought to be!

We would not come running into the house as if Jerry just hollered, "Get in here! Mom is now serving hot fudge sundaes!" No, it was not like that. Prayer is not necessarily meant to be like mealtime. (Only in respect to being a daily thing we are called to do.) Neither was it like when we played Monopoly or other board games, which we often did. Family prayer was sacred without being a hardship to me or my siblings. It was and still is a very special memory I will always cherish.

Pray is holy. It is solemn, sacred, and a time of reverence. Plus, our parents did not use prayer time to scold us, teach some Bible lesson, or lecture us regarding its importance. We just prayed. In doing so, Mother and Dad led by example. We also knew family prayer time was not the only time our parents prayed, for we heard them often in their room and in Dad's study as he prayerfully prepared sermons for church.

We were not allowed to bring home our neighborhood friends on Thursdays. That was the day my father studied for his Sunday sermons, and he would spend time in prayer—prayers heard throughout our house. But one Thursday when I was around ten years old, I ran into the house to get my baseball glove. I was not aware that my buddy followed me inside. I ran upstairs, got the glove, and ran down the steps. My friend stood frozen as if he had seen a ghost. I immediately knew what the problem was. He didn't see a ghost. He was hearing my father praying in the Holy Ghost! I said to my friend, "Come on. That's just my dad praying." That sound that completely spooked my friend was the most normal sound to me. Prayer, even Holy Ghost prayer, is what happened in our home and in the lives of the Wilkerson's.

As I grew older, I saw prayer more than just a duty, but also a delight. Here's the reason why. When we prayed, there usually was a focus on seeking God for something specific. If one of us were sick, we were prayed for. When someone in the church lost a loved one, we prayed for them in their grief. A frequent prayer was praying for "our daily bread," and in our case, bread meant the money needed to meet the household budget. There were no financial surpluses in the Wilkerson household. As Dad often said, *"We live from hand to mouth, from God's hand to our mouth."* Pray was an essential part of our lives, both spiritually and materially.

Our family prayer times were filled with specific requests. When the specific answers came— and they came often and in miraculous ways—our faith was strengthened, making prayer time very significant and exciting. We knew we were not just saying words. We knew we were praying to the living God, and we expected Him to *"supply all our needs,"* a promise in His Word that we could bank on (Philippians 4:19).

In this manner, prayer became much more than a duty, but also a great delight. Prayer is what made everything else we did meaningful. It was the central thing in our lives; not just because of the frequency of our prayers, but what happened as a result. Prayer is about Who, not just about what! Just as marriage is about who we love, who we are committed to, and who we enjoy being with. Yes, prayer, just like a marriage, can get stale and monotonous at times. It doesn't mean you give up on the marriage any more than if the same thing happens in one's prayer life. We keep praying because we love God, we love Jesus.

> Prayer is the means that God has of knowing that we are ready to receive what He wants us to have. — A.W. Tozer[13]

Song 4
Draw Me Nearer

I am Thine, O Lord
I have heard Thy voice
And it told Thy love for me
But I long to raise in the arms of faith
And be closer drawn to Thee

Draw me nearer, nearer, nearer, blessed Lord
To the cross where Thou hast died
Draw me nearer, nearer, neared, blessed Lord
To Thy bleeding side

Consecrate me now to Thy service, Lord
By the pow'r of grace divine
Let my soul look up with steadfast hope
And my will lost in Thine

Oh, the pure delight of a single hour
That before Thy throne I spend
When I kneel in prayer, and with Thee, my God
I commune as friend with friend

There are depths of love that I cannot know
Till I cross the narrow sea;
There are heights of joy that I may not reach
Till I rest in peace with Thee[14]

4
DESIRE

A lmost all things in life are obtained by desire. When looking for synonyms for this word "desire" what comes up is *want, wish, crave, covet.* I would add the word *longing.* As the word "desire" applies to prayer, it is a prerequisite to desire to have a consistent prayer life. Almost all things worth wanting to have or do in life are accomplished through desire.

Prayer without desire is like losing one's appetite while at the dinner table. Desire can apply to wanting God to grant us an answer to a specific need, to a personal need, or any other request in the form of a blessing for ourselves or another.

Desire turns a passive prayer into a passionate one. E.M. Bounds writes:

> Desire is not merely a simple wish; it is a deep-seated craving; an intense longing for attainment. In the realm of spiritual affairs, it is important adjunct to prayer. So important it is, that one may almost say, almost, that desire is an absolute essential to prayer. Desire precedes prayer, accompanies it, is followed by it. Desire goes before prayer, and, by it, is created and intensified. Payer is the oral

expression of desire. If prayer is asking God for something, then prayer must be expressed. Prayer comes out into the open. Desire is silent prayer. Prayer is heard, desire unheard. The deeper the desire, the stronger the prayer. Without desire, prayer is a meaningless jumble of words. Such perfunctory, formal prayer, with no heart, no feeling, no real desire accompanying it, is to be shunned like a pestilence. Its exercise is a waste of precious time, and from it, no real blessings accrue.[15]

Desires, of course, can be fleshly and sinful. Right desires should be at the root of all prayers.

I recall as a teenager just getting serious about Bible reading and studying, and how I was blessed by a verse of Scripture that, at first, I misunderstood. It is Psalm 37:4 which states:

Delight yourself also in the Lord, and He shall give you the desires of your heart.

At first, this was a wonderful promise to me, sort of like an ATM card in which I didn't even need to make bank deposits because the Lord would do it for me. But as a teen, I was discovering desires I never had before that gave me pause in claiming the promise of Psalm 34:7. As is sometimes the case, in grabbing ahold of a verse of Scripture and running with it, we sometimes fail to read it in context. When I read the next verse, Psalm 37:5, only then did I see the true meaning of God giving us the desires of our heart. The next verse says,

> Commit your way to the Lord, trust also in Him. And He shall bring it to pass.

When we surrender to God's will, our prayers are then sanctified and come in alignment with His Word and will. Without commitment and trust in God, our desires fulfilled can ruin our spiritual health.

Desire, like hunger, should prompt within us a sense of need. The deeper the need, the deeper and more active will be our prayers. Motivated by need, prayer should be a longing for something of which we do not yet possess, and it can just as well be something in the natural or supernatural. There is a heaven-given appetite of which Jesus said,

> They that hunger and thirst for righteousness shall be filled (Matt. 5:6).

When we have this, it is proof of a renewed heart that is delighting in the Lord. E.M. Bounds further writes:

> Physical appetites are the attributes of a living body, not a corpse, and spiritual desires belong to a soul made alive to God. And as the renewed soul hungers after righteousness, these holy inward desires break out into earnest supplicating prayer.[16]

ABOUT PRAYER!

When desire is lacking, prayer is lacking. And when our desires are more for natural things—be they secular or sacred, business or domestic, or even legitimate activates—prayer can take second, third, or no place at all in our daily schedule. Holy desire become the flame that will ignite our prayer life.

Spiritual desire must be born in us as we are born-again in Christ. It's amazing how our desires change, or should change, as a result of the new birth. However, it has been my experience when a person comes to Christ from a background of drug addiction, alcoholism or some other life controlling problem and they really want a new life, that desire draws them to God in prayer. But once saved, the prayer desires are not the same after they are living a new life. They are sometimes like what John wrote in the book of Revelation to the church at Ephesus:

Nevertheless I have this against you, that you have left your first love (Rev. 2:4).

I write *About Prayer* primarily to new believers and especially those who have come to Christ in a faith-based, Christ-centered, discipleship-rehab program. Have you lost your First Love? How often do you practice daily prayer, driven by godly desires?

One of my favorite verses in the Psalms motivated me as a teenager to follow Jesus' instructions to find a private place for focused prayer. I literally did so in our parsonage in Scranton, Pennsylvania on Greenwich Avenue for this one main reason:

One thing have I desired of the Lord, that will I seek; that I may dwell in the house of the Lord all the days of my life, to behold the beauty of the Lord, and to inquire in His temple (Psalm 27:4).

Hunger is what draws us to where food is. In like manner, the inward consciousness of our spiritual need draws us to the place of prayer. It is a longing for something we do not have, that we do not yet possess, but which God has promised. Isaiah prayed,

The desire of our soul is for Your name and for the remembrance of Your name (Isaiah 26:8).

I've been embarrassed numerous times when seeing someone I've met before, sometimes quite a few times, and I don't remember their name. How embarrassing! How must God feel when we forget His name in prayer.

Proverbs 13:19 says, *"A desire accomplished is sweet to the soul."* I recall when I'd come out of the prayer closet of my bedroom, that verse in Proverbs was a reality to me. My time of prayer once accomplished was sweet to my soul.

I don't remember my father saying anything about me developing a prayer life at such an early age. That I believe was because following in the footsteps of praying parents was something that was assumed would happen to the offspring of Kenneth and Ann

Wilkerson. Prayer became to us kids both a duty and a delight.

A further quote of E.M. Bounds in this regard to this is:

The absence of this holy desire in the heart is a presumptive proof, either of a decline in spiritual ecstasy, or, that the new birth has never taken place. They that hunger and thirst after righteousness, they shall be filled... Desire is the will in action, a strong conscious longing, excited in the inner nature, for some great good. Desire exalts the object of its longing and fixes its mind on it.[17]

Song 5
This is My Desire

This is my desire, to honor You
Lord, with all my heart, I worship You
All I have within me, I give You praise
All that I adore is in You

Lord, I give you my heart
I give you my soul, I live for You alone
Every breath that I take, every moment I'm awake
Lord, have Your way in me

And I will live
And I will live
And I will live for You

Lord, I give you my heart
I give you my soul, I live for You alone
Every breath that I take, every moment I'm awake
Lord, have Your way in me[18]

5

DESPERATION

In my desperation I prayed, and the Lord listened; he saved me from all my troubles.
(Psalm 34:6 NLT)

On one occasion when I was Director-Pastor in a faith-based rehab ministry, I noticed that a student-resident in our program was an outstanding seeker after God who answered every single altar call. It was reported to me that he'd often go to our basement weight room when empty to pray. I asked him one day if he grew up in church.

He replied, "My family was Catholic, and we went to church only occasionally."

I asked, "How and where did you learn to pray?"

He gave me a strange answer. "I learned how to pray from my street life when I was coping drugs."

"How so?" I responded.

"Well, Pastor," he said with a smile, "I learned on the streets all about desperation. I was desperate to get high. At times, I'd stand shivering in a winter storm, waiting for my drug connection to show up. Other times, even in the pouring rain, I would persevere until my drug connection arrived. I learned desperation on the streets. So, when I came here, I wanted to get clean and live a normal, drug-free life. Somehow, I knew if I could in the past be so dedicated to getting high, I needed to take that same desire for drugs and redirect it to connect with God instead. Since I was so desperate for drugs, why not find an answer to my drug problem by pursuing God in prayer with the same desperation?"

I walked away knowing I had just been given one of the wisest lessons on prayer, although based on street wisdom.

Then I remembered that Jesus once taught a lesson using an unusual parable that was similar in nature to this newborn addict's situation, following the foresight and shrewdness of a dishonest person. He did so out of desperation to survive, but we seek to increase our spiritual wealth through prayer. The parable Jesus taught is entitled *The Parable of the Shrewd Manager*. It's about a money manager who was losing his job, so he devised a way to survive by going to his Master's debtors, saying that he was representing his master and reducing their debts. In so doing, he was able to collect a partial amount owed to his master and make some friends who would give him a place to live after losing his livelihood. The Scriptures say, *"The Master commended the dishonest manager because he acted shrewdly"* (Luke 16:8).

Jesus was giving a lesson on the proper and improper use of money and the importance and responsibility of money management. What at first seems to be Jesus condoning cheating and dishonesty, turns out to be a lesson in using money responsibly and with integrity and foresight.

A more subtle lesson relates to what I learned about prayer from a former street addict. That is, we ought to use wisely our investment of money in a way that will be a blessing to others. Prayer, like money, requires the responsible use of it to gain eternal rewards. The street addict mentioned above turned one kind of destructive desperation into a better kind, directing his desperation towards something good, holy, and life changing.

In *The Message* translation in this parable, in verses 8 and 9, Jesus uses the same kind of lesson about the wise use of money as the above illustration about prayer given by an ex-drug addict. Eugene Peterson writes:

> Now here's a surprise: The master praised the crooked manager! And why? Because he knew how to look after himself. Streetwise people are smarter in this regard than law-abiding citizens. They are constantly alert, looking for angles, surviving by their wits. I want you to be smart in the same way — [such as in prayer, I might add] — but for what is right — using every adversity to stimulate your creative survival, to consecrate your attention on the bare

essentials, so you'll live, really live, and not complacently just get by on good behavior.

In other words, sometimes the world is better at doing what is not good than believers are at doing good. Desperation prayers to a Higher Power enables the one who prays to reach higher goals.

When I was researching about the definition of the word "delight," in one source it gave the following synonyms: "covet, crave, hunger, lust, long, pant, yearn and desperation." That last one is a word I well understood when working so many years with drug addicts. They lived hopeless lives, having both society and the medical profession telling them they had a lifetime disease from which they could never recover.

I, in turn, and those in the faith-based community taught that it does not matter if addiction is called a habit, a disease, or whatever. Even if it is a disease, it's a curable disease for Jesus. We base this on the Bible verse in 2 Corinthians 5:17 which proclaims,

> Therefore, if anyone is in Christ, he is a new creation; old things have passed away; behold all things have become new.

However, for this promise to become a reality, the addict must be desperate for help, desperate to be committed to a program that can help them, a desperation expressed in prayer as a seeker after God. While speaking and preaching to addicts, I would tell them that there is a difference between wanting to get clean and wanting to get cured. Getting clean is like going through a car wash. After a few minutes of that water wash, the car is clean. But you know your car is going to get dirty again.

Short term detox programs are like that car wash. Addicts need a new engine—a new heart, and not just a temporary, outward cleansing. But it takes a call, a cry, a prayer of desperation to experience 2 Corinthians 5:17. This is true for new believers as well. Romans 3:23 says that all have sinned and fallen short of the glory of God, all are in need of a passionate new heart after God's own heart.

Passionless prayer has no heart in it—no desperation. *"The effectual fervent prayer of a righteous man availeth much,"* James 5:16 says. In the sports world I have heard coaches on the losing side say, *"I guess we didn't want the win as much as our opponent did."* Passion and desperation tip the scales between winning and losing in many natural things as well as in prayer.

He prays not at all, when he does not press his need. —E.M. Bounds[19]

It's my personal experience that we can start out red hot in prayer and then become faint-hearted. This is why when Jesus gave a lesson on the importance of passion and persistence in prayer that he prefaced it by saying, *"Men ought always to pray, and not to faint"* (Luke 18:1). He added *"not to faint"* because Jesus knew that prayer requires a discipline of alertness, concentration, and single-mindedness. The enemy of the believer's prayer life seeks to create distractions.

They come in the form of sudden physical weariness, interruptions of various sorts, and sometimes what is clearly a Satanic attack.

Someone once told me that if I forgot to do something, the best way to remember was to begin to pray. With tongue-in-cheek he added, "The devil will surely remind you because he does not want saints to pray. If anyone knows the power of prayer, it's Satan."

> Our hearts need much to be worked over, not only to get the evil out of them, but to get the good in them. —E.M. Bounds[20]

> There is so much against our prayer life. For me, the enemy of our soul despises the power of prayer, and with everything he can muster will discourage our prayer life. —A.W. Tozer[21]

6

PETITIONING THE COURT

He who judges me is the Lord.
(1 Corinthians 4:4)

We know the disciples asked Jesus to teach them about prayer (Luke 11:1), and in answering, Jesus gives a picture of prayer and Himself in three different character stories. One story is about a "friend" asking another friend for three loaves of bread at midnight. In the second story, Jesus refers to Himself as a caring and giving "father." The third one is not told in a parable, but in a story that follows in Luke 11:14-23 about demons being cast out of a man. In that case, Jesus is illustrated as a "strong man."

These three portrayals of Jesus in relation to prayer—friend, father, and strong man—convey truth that denotes the importance of access to God in prayer, and that there is power in prayer. For example, Jesus says,

> When a strong man is fully armed and guards his palace, his possessions are safe—until someone stronger attacks and overpowers him, strips him of his weapons, and carries off his belongings (Luke 11:21-22).

There is another way of seeing God; that is, as a Judge. Seeing God as a Judge means we can enter His court to petition Him, the Judge of the universe, in prayer for our needs because he has the power to render favorably a decision in respect to our petition. We do not readily see God as Judge since that typically conveys images of judgement: as Hebrews 10:31 says, *"It is a fearful thing to fall into the hands of the living God,"* especially if He is our Judge. And to be sure, among of all His names and purposes, God is a Judge as the following Scriptures state:

- He shall judge the world in righteousness, and He shall administer judgment for the peoples of the earth (Psalm 9:8).

- Gather My saints together to Me, those who have made a covenant with Me by sacrifice. Let the heavens declare His righteousness, for God Himself is Judge (Psalm 50:6).

- In the day when God will judge the secrets of men by Jesus Christ, according to my gospel (Romans 2:16).

- Tell the nations, "The Lord reigns." The world stands firm and cannot be shaken, He will judge all peoples fairly (Psalm 96:11).

In my ministry I have dealt with an unusual number of those seeking help from a life-controlling problem who have had cases in court. I therefore do write to those who understand what it means to stand before a Judge. Most of the cases were merely to hear a sentence announced against them.

I feel in writing about *A Beginner's Guide* on prayer that describing it as if it were a case in court might be helpful to all readers, whether you have been called to court to stand before a Judge or not. I assume most of you haven't, but you've probably seen a TV show or movie depicting a courtroom case. Personally, I always love watching such shows.

Most of us as believers do not readily want to view God as a Judge. Rather, we want to see Him as Creator, Forgiver of Sins, the All-Powerful One, the Ruler of the Nations, and other inviting images of His many attributes. But make no mistake; God is a Judge. The verse that used to scare me to my core as I grew up in church is 2 Corinthians 5:10:

> For we must all appear before the judgement seat of Christ, that each one may receive the things done in the body.

This truth drove me to the altar on numerous occasions.

From the beginning of time, God has been portrayed as a Judge. The first reference is when Abram was promised that his seed, the Israelites, would serve in a strange land and *"that nation, whom they shall serve, will I judge"* (Genesis 15:13-14).

Psalm 50:3-4 says, *"Our God comes and will not be silent…. He summons the heaven above, and the earth, that he may judge his people."*

Hebrews 12:23 refers to *"God the judge of all."*

Hebrews 10:30-31 says, *"The Lord will judge his people. It is a fearful thing to fall into the hands of the living God."*

God, as a Judge in a courtroom, does not inspire us as much as God our Father, God the Almighty, the God of love, mercy, and grace. But it is clear in Scripture that God cannot be known in all His attributes apart from also being Judge, now and in the future. If you are not a believer, the fact that God is the Judge of the universe and the nations ought to cause you to immediately bow in humility and cry out for forgiveness of your sins.

The good thing for believers is that since God is a Judge, He is the one that we can petition to as we seek answers to our prayer. As we come to God, recognizing Him as Judge, we can engage Him in what I call Courtroom prayers.

Here is what we can learn about "Petitioning the Court," making known our case in prayer:

1. Enter His courts with the password, "Thank You!"

Psalm 100:4 says, *"Enter his gates with thanksgiving, And into His courts with praise. Be thankful to Him, and bless*

His name." The Message renders this verse as *"Enter with the password: "Thank you!"*

Earthly courts are ominous, presenting an image of fear as we enter its doors and see the robed Judge taking his or her place behind the bench to hear the next case. Even the bench itself is a fearful image.

It's much different in the courtroom of God where we are invited to come and present our petitions in prayer. We can enter with a heart full of praise because our guilt has been absorbed and paid for on the cross. We are in good standing in this courtroom because of the payment of Another, the Judge's only Son! We have a right to stand before God because of the righteousness of Christ graciously imparted to us. No wonder the Psalmist says to *"Enter His gates with thanksgiving and into His courts with praise"* (Psalm 100:4).

In the courtroom of prayer, it's not a matter innocence or guilt, because that has already been settled. It's a matter of...does what we're asking line up with the promises of God. If we petition for bread, God will not give us a rock. If we petition for a fish, He'll not give us a snake. Courtroom prayers are in my estimation one of the best and easiest ways to get an answer. I'd like to look at three things regarding them.

2. The Scripture is clear as to who has petition rights in the Courtroom of God and who does not.

Psalm 54:1-2 says (KJV) *"Save me, O God, by thy name, and judge me by thy strength. Hear my prayer, O God; give ear to the words of my mouth."* As a blood-bought son of God, you have standing in the Courtroom of Prayer. Isaiah 43:26 (CEV) states: *"Meet me in court! State your case and prove you are right."* In this courtroom of prayer, you do not need to show up with evidence of "good works" to boast about. You don't need letters of recommendation from your pastor or spiritual leader. You do not need to prove you have a right to petition the court for an answer to your prayer by showing up with a bunch of witnesses that say you are a good guy or girl. All you need is for the courtroom clerk to see if your name is listed in *"the Lamb's Book of Life"* (Revelation 21:27).

Courtroom prayers have a scriptural basis and therefore it is something we should practice. If you can understand this at the outset of your walk with God, your prayers and prayer life will result in numerous answers to prayer and God's blessings on your life. In fact, you can come boldly and bravely *"before the throne [and the Judge's bench] of our merciful God. There we will be treated with underserving grace, and we will find help"* (Hebrews 4:16 CEV).

3. If you seek justice for a case brought against you unjustly by anyone in the body of Christ (including a pastor, leader, ministry CEO, or any other person this is also the purpose of courtroom prayers.

Almost weekly I read from Christian news sources of a pastor/leader accused in various ways of violating biblical conduct: being too controlling, being emotionally, verbally, or even sexually abusive. I know there are often two sides to this. The accused can be innocent and/or the victim innocent of any wrongdoing. In either case, what does one or the other party do? Sometimes there is no ecclesiastical court in which to try such a case. When no solution can be found for injustice, people say, *"Leave it in the hands of the Lord."* But that does not heal the hurt.

It's also easy to say, *"Pray about it."* Neither is that satisfactory to most. But in the end, we must leave the matter in the hands of the Supreme Court of heaven which will always (ultimately) render a perfect verdict. Sometimes He does this now and openly and we know about it. Sometimes God is working behind the scenes bringing judgement on the guilty, although the accuser or accusers may not know about it.

The only way one can deal with an injustice in the end is to trust God as Judge in how He renders what may be a sealed verdict. I have watched friends make huge unbiblical responses to either their mistakes or the mistakes of others — and bring much harm to the body of Christ, especially spiritually weak brothers and sisters. When a severe injustice is done to someone, this can be a deep hurt which can often last a lifetime. Yet, the Scriptures are clear:

> Dear friends, never take revenge. Leave that to the righteous anger of God. For the

Scripture says, "I will take revenge; I will pay them back, says the Lord" (Romans 12:19 NLT).

4. Is there a time to go to before God as Judge when you know your guilty of a wrong, a sin?

As has been stated, the concept of the courtroom of prayer is that by the shed blood of Jesus our sin and sins are blotted out. I know individuals who have gone to court for a crime they committed, and they had a long record of previous crimes. But in God's courtroom there is no past record of our sins as the song says, *"My sins are blotted out, I know!"*[22]

I wrote in my *Challenge Study Bible* on Isaiah 43:24 (CEV): *"But I wipe away your sins because of who I am. And so, I will forget the wrongs you have done."* The next verse then says, *"Meet me in court! State your case and prove you are right."* This was written to God's people the Israelites who had not been honoring the Lord. Yet in the midst of pointing out that they had been *"burden[ed] down with you [for their] terrible sins"* (Isaiah 43:24) was the promise of a restart of a walk of forgiveness and holiness before God.[23]

In the New Testament, regarding someone who relapses, John the Apostle wrote, *"...so you may not sin. And if anyone sins, we have an Advocate with the Father, Jesus Christ the righteous"* (I John 2:1).

As previously written, when viewing prayer as if going with a petition to God the Judge, Jesus declared, *"If you ask anything in My name, I will do it"* (John 14:14). This is based on having the right to petition because the grace and mercy of God has raised us up to *"sit in heaven places in Christ Jesus"* (Ephesians 2:8). However, going before God when we have sinned needs to be a prayer of confession, godly sorrow, and humility. Thankfully, the courtroom of prayer is open to petition Father God in the name of Jesus Christ for *"anything"* including when having sinned as one of God's children.

5. There can come a time in presenting a prayer petition to Father-God and Father-Judge that you may need to do what is done in a regular court, that is, to ask to approach the bench.

You've probably seen in a TV courtroom drama when an attorney will ask the Judge, "May I approach the bench?" Usually, the Judge will indicate by sign language that he allows it. And it is so when "approaching the bench" in our prayers to God. When we do so, it's good to bear in mind two Scriptures: The first one is Isaiah 54:5:

> The Lord All-Powerful, the Holy God of Israel, rules all the earth. He is your Creator and husband, and he will rescue you (CEV).

This All-Powerful Ruler of the earth is not out to get us, but to rescue us! We can approach His bench if and when we have sinned because God is both our Judge and our Advocate, as 1 John 2:1-2 says:

> My little children, these things I write to you, so that you may not sin. And if anyone sins, we have an Advocate with the Father, Jesus Christ the righteous. And He Himself is the propitiation for our sins, and not for ours only but also for the whole world.

Song 6
Standing on the Promises

Standing on the promises of Christ, my King
Through eternal ages let His praises ring
Glory in the highest, I will shout and sing
Standing on the promises of God

Standing, standing,
Standing on the promises of God, my Savior
Standing, standing,
I'm standing on the promises of God

Standing on the promises that cannot fail
When the howling storms of doubt and fear assail
By the living Word of God I shall prevail
Standing on the promises of God.

Standing on the promises of Christ, the Lord
Bound to Him eternally by love's strong cord
Overcoming daily with the Spirit's sword
Standing on the promises of God. [Refrain]

Standing on the promises I cannot fall
List'ning ev'ry moment to the Spirit's call
Resting in my Savior as my all in all,
Standing on the promises of God.[24]

7

PRAYER AND THE PROMISES OF GOD

**You don't have what you want
because you don't ask for it.**
(James 4:2 NLT)

One of the worst things about not praying is what we miss out on as a result. God has so much for us that we do not claim. I once went to ask a philanthropist to ask for a grant in the amount of $150,000. He said, "Where do I send the check?" That was it. No further questions asked. I left the office feeling like I could have asked for more, but I did not. Fortunately, he decided without my asking to send double the amount. God often does the same (Read Ephesians 3:20).

We often go to God underestimating His willingness to answer our petitions. I honestly have never fully grasped the promise that *"If you ask anything in My name, I will do it"* (John 14:14). What is the range within which we can ask something of God and from God? *"Anything."* What a promise! What a responsibility!

Jesus could not have made it clearer on the importance of asking in prayer and particularly, among other things, He wants us to claim His promises. How foolish it would be to withdraw only a small portion of funds from a bank with unlimited funds when you really need much more. It is estimated there are some 800 promises in the New Testament and that doesn't include the ones found in the Old Testament, too.

I heard of someone who went to heaven and were given a tour. They passed a room full of gifts. When they asked what the unopened gifts represented, the heavenly tour guide said, "Those are all the unclaimed gifts believers could have had but they never asked for them."

There are many things in life we cheat ourselves out of because we do not pursue them for various reasons such as slothfulness, indifference, and being satisfied with less. This is certainly the case when it comes to prayer.

Paul prayed for the brethren in Colossae, sharing that he *"did not cease to pray"* for them and among other things he *"gave thanks to the Father who has qualified us to be partakers of the inheritance of the saints in light."* (Colossians 1: 9, 12) In prayer, we have access to our inheritance in Christ.

Psalm 121:1 says,

I will lift up my eyes to the hills, from whence come my help.

Hills and mountains in the Bible represent higher ground and a higher place in God that brings blessings not obtained in the lowlands of our Christian walk. Psalm 104 is a wonderful description of the things God has prepared for us in nature. Verse 13 is applicable to claiming higher and better things from God: *"He waters the hills from His upper chambers."* Those that hunger and thirst for more of God must go higher to satisfy that thirst. The best things of God are, spiritually speaking, in the higher places through prayer.

The Promises of God are so vast, so great and mighty it's hard to select the best. Most believers who have a daily and consistent prayer life precede prayer with Bible reading or, as I write elsewhere, they incorporate Scripture in their prayers. Psalm 2:6 says, *"God set His king "On my holy hill."* If you want to be near Him, then in faith, draw near to God and He will draw near to you. (James 4:8)

I challenge you to search the Scriptures and list at least ten of your favorite promises from God. Here are mine:

1. THE PROMISE OF THE BLOOD!

"But now in Christ Jesus you who were once afar off have been brought near by the blood of Christ" (Ephesians 2:13. Reading Ephesians Chapter 2 is a great preparation for prayer.) There is no remission of sins apart from the shed blood of Christ. (See Hebrews 9:22)

I wrote the following commentary on Hebrews 9:22 in my *Challenge Study Bible* relative to this promise:

"IF GOD DOES NOT REMEMBER OUR SINS, NEITHER SHOULD YOU. The once-a-year ritual when the High Priest [in the Old Testament] entered the Most Holy Place to offer atonement for sin was called the Day of Atonement. There was a temporary feeling of forgiveness, but their guilt was not [entirely] gone, because they knew they had to return again and again to offer a sacrifice. Hebrews Chapter 10 talks about the perfect sacrifice of Christ by which we have been purified [and saved] once and for all." Oh, what a promise! In the new life and in prayer everything starts at the cross.[25]

2. THE PROMISE OF "ACCESS" TO GOD!

What follows after the cross and in the possibilities in prayer is because of this beautiful word "access."

Ephesians 5:2 says, *"Through whom also we have access by faith into this grace in which we stand and rejoice in the hope of the glory of God."* In addition, Ephesians 2:18 declares: *"For though Him we both have access by one Spirit to the Father."*

The word *"access"* as it relates to pray, is one of my favorite words and promises.

It follows that when Christ gave His blood by His death on the cross, we have this wonderful promise of access to God the Father though the Son. Sin denies us access. One of the most awesome Scriptures early in the Bible was in the time of Noah when the flood covered the earth and the Word says,

"When they were all in the boat, the Lord closed the door" (Genesis 7:16).

Imagine the door of heaven shut to you because you have not taken hold of the promise of being in the Ark of Salvation. Another commentary from the *Challenge Study Bible* on the shut door of salvation is:

"AND THE DOOR WAS SHUT [what awesome words]. The possibility of salvation for Noah's generation lasted 120 years. Every pound of the hammer by Noah and his sons, every swing of the ax [in the building of the Ark] was another opportunity for mankind to repent."[26]

They did not! Which side of the door of salvation are you on? The door is open. Christ is now our Ark of Salvation through Whom we have safety and security: *"Let us come boldly unto the throne of grace, that we may obtain mercy and find grace to help in time of need"* (Hebrews 4:16).

My pastor father used to tell the story of a woman on board a ship from New York to London. Every mealtime she would never enter the dining hall to eat. She'd go and stand on the outer deck. After observing her for several days, a ship's steward asked her why she never ate a meal. She answered, "Oh, I bought a ticket just as a passenger. I could not afford the meal ticket, also." The steward said, "Let me see your ticket." He looked at it and smiled, saying, "This is a First-Class ticket. It entitles you to eat every meal. Go ahead in right now and enjoy your meal today and every day on the way to London."

She had *access* to a dining area full of delicious food and didn't even know it. What a shame that more believers do not know that all the promises of God are available just for the asking.

3. THE PROMISE OF "THINGS"

The Bible says, *"One's life does not consist in the abundance of the things he possesses"* (Luke 12:15). These are the words of Jesus. At another time and place He also said in respect to having the physical necessities in life that *"All these things shall be added unto to you"* (Matthew 6:33). Obviously, there are sinful things, lustful things, good things, bad things, and natural "things." Jesus said we should not worry about natural things such as food and health because *"Your Father knows that you need all these things"* (Matthew 6:32).

I was raised in the church and in a pastor's home where we did not have a lot of "things," whether necessities or acceptable pleasures. Our parents stood on the promise of Matthew 6:33. When my pastor/father changed churches, my sister had an opportunity for a university scholarship which she gave up to help work in the new church where we moved. I recall her testifying in a service that she was going to stand on the promise of Matthew 6:33: *"But seek first the kingdom of God and His righteousness and all these things shall be added unto you."* We took it to mean God putting food on the table, helping our family pay bills; even such things as prospects of marriage, a job, better pay, healing, and other things that lined up with the promises of God.

> Therefore, I say to you, whatever things you ask when you pray, believe that you receive them, and you will have them (Mark 11:24).

"You will have them." What a promise to claim!

4. THE PROMISE "KEEPER"

In His prayer to His Father as quoted in John chapter 17:6, Jesus said,

> I have manifested Your name to the men which You have given me out of the world. They were Yours. You gave them to me, and they have kept Your word.

"Kept Your word." That is the promise we are to hold on to. This gives us access to press our needs to our Father in heaven. The other part of the promise is God's promising through His Son to *"keep"* us. The other part of Jesus prayer in John 17 is this:

> I kept them in Your name. Those you have given Me I have kept (John 17:12).

In some churches, at the conclusion of the service, there is a Scripture reading called the Doxology. It is a promise that, as the church people leave the service and go out to live their lives in the world, the Word of God promises us this: *"Unto Him that is able to keep you from falling…"* (Jude 24)

5. THE PROMISE OF ABUNDANCE!

I have come that they may have life, and that they may have it more abundantly (John 10:10).

There is a definition of abundance that has to do with material things but for the believer it primarily applies to spiritual things, but not exclusively. Paul writes to the church at Phillipi: *"For all seek their own, not the things that which of are of Christ Jesus"* (2:21). Yet when all the Scriptures are considered, we find God does bless some materially. If God has given you a talent, a gifting, either naturally or supernaturally, and you prosper financially be responsible with what you're given in a godly way.

Most usage of abundance and prosperity in Scripture has to do with spiritual blessings such as asking for one of the spiritual gifts to bring honor and glory to God. In this regard, I have made my number one prayer request to get more wisdom, guidance, discernment, and other things on a needed basis. Other related requests could be to forgive others, loving someone hard to love, carrying prayer burdens for those ones in need. Yet "abundance" can also apply to earthly and natural things: *"According to your faith let it be to you"* (Matthew 9:29). Ephesians 3:23 is one of the God promises that can be applied more broadly:

Now to Him who is able to do exceedingly abundantly above all we can ask or think, according to the power that works in us.

You might want to underline that promise in your personal Bible!

Many believers are satisfied to just be saved with the assurance that when they die, they will go to heaven. They do not seek for more. Most pastors challenge their church members to seek for more of God, and the fact that many do not, is one of the things that most distresses them. Any parent who has a child who does not reach their full potential distresses them; so it is with spiritual fathers. Leaders want the children of God not to be just spectators, lukewarm Christians, or a number to be counted on a list of church service attenders.

In Psalm 115:14 the writer prays, "*May the Lord increase you more and more.*" Paul prayed for the believers in Thessalonica that "*You should abound more and more*" (1 Thessalonians 4:1). He was referring to their walk with God and this refers indirectly to their prayer life and ours.

6. THE PROMISE OF GUIDANCE!

This has to do with finding the will of God personally for our lives: the choice of a college or university, the choice of a spouse, where to worship, what career or job to choose, where to live, etc. I have found there are some things God trusts us to make our own decisions on. For example, we'd like His witness on what home, car, or other things in life to get, but He may or may not indicate to us what choice to make.

Many struggle with finding God's will. He does promise guidance, but we don't need to wake up in the morning and pray about which clothes to put on or what kind of breakfast food to eat. "Lord, is it Raisin Bran or oatmeal today?" But in the larger things in life, the promise is: *"This is God, our God forever and ever; He will be our guide even to death"* (Psalm 48:14).

7. THE PROMISE OF THE HEATHEN!

Ask of me, and I shall give thee the heathen [most other translations use the word nations for heathen] for thine inheritance, and the uttermost part of the earth for thy possession (Psalm 2:8 KJV).

This appears to be an unusual promise to choose, but not when its full meaning is unfolded. The previous verse, Psalm 2:7 says, *I will declare the decree: The Lord has said to Me, "You are My Son, today I have begotten You."* Just as God so loved the world that He gave His only begotten son and if you believe in Him and He saved you, you can, in turn, ask Him to save an unsaved person before they are sentenced to eternal separation from Him.

This is a promise for missionaries, for a saved member of a household praying for unsaved members, for friends that we are burdened over to come to Christ. This is a promise that extends to a saved spouse praying for an unsaved one in a marriage and extends to the *"uttermost parts of the earth"* and everyone in between who need salvation.

8. THE PROMISE OF THE CHAIN BREAKER

God rescued us from dead-end alleys and dark dungeons. He set us up in the kingdom of the Son he loves so much the Son who got us out of the pit we were in, got rid of the sins we were doomed to keep repeating (Colossians 1:13-14 The Message).

The Bible says, *"All have sinned"* but not everyone sins in the same way. Some are bound in heavy chains, chains of addictions and other sin-controlling ways. For some, deliverance is instantaneous; for most it's a process, a process that best happens when the person in need goes into a long-term, rehab-discipleship program. This provides the ingredients necessary for lasting change: The Word, the Holy Spirit, worship, prayer, encouragement, accountable and counseling.

There is no way better to understand this promise than for me to share the lyrics of the song, *He's a Chain Breaker* which I will add at the end of this chapter.

9. THE PROMISE OF 29:11
THE JEREMIAH CODE

I wrote a book entitled *29:11 The Jeremiah Code.*[27] It is based on a well-known and favorite Scripture to many believers which says,

> For I know the plans I have for you, declares the Lord, plans to prosper you and not to harm you, plans to give you hope and a future.

> The NLT says, They are plans for good and not for disaster, to give you a future and a hope.

> This is one of the most popular and most quoted verse among believers. In my book, I show how while the children of Israel were experiencing many great trails and testing, this promise became like a beam of light in a time of darkness. It continues to have wonderful application for us today.

10. THE PROMISE OF REST

We say of someone who has died, "May he or she rest in peace." I suppose death is a rest from the hustle, bustle, hassle, trouble, hurriedness, and other stresses of being alive. I have retired twice in my lifetime. After the first, I was called out of the bullpen of leadership to take the mound again and try to lead my team to victory. I'm not sure if I succeeded. It would be twelve more years before I could really retire.

Am I resting now? Yes, as to one of the meanings of rest. I rest my body more now. My mind? Well, that's another thing. There is a resting of faith that enable us to cast all our cares on Him. In this faith-rest we are free from stress, anxiety, and anxiousness. Augustine wrote in *Confessions,*

> Thou hast made us for Thyself, O Lord, and our hearts are restless until they rest in Thee.[28]

Song 7
He's A Chain Breaker

If you've been walking the same old road
For miles and miles
If you've been hearing the same old voice
Tell the same old lies
If you're trying to fill the same old holes inside
There's a better life, there's a better life

If you've got pain, He's a pain taker
If you feel lost, He's a way maker
If you need freedom or saving
He's a prison-shaking Saviour
If you got chains
He's a chain breaker

We've all searched for the light of day
In the dead of night
We've all found ourselves worn out
From the same old fight
We've all run to things we know just ain't right
When there's a better life, there's a better life

If you believe it, if you receive it
If you can feel it, somebody testify
If you believe it, if you receive it
If you can feel it, somebody testify, testify.[29]

8

PRACTICAL AIDS FOR DAILY PRAYER

Lord, teach us to pray.
(Luke 11:1)

Sometimes we can get too spiritual in preaching, teaching, and writing about prayer by neglecting to lay out practical guidelines about when, how, and what to pray for. I have known those who read about accounts of people who prayed very long hours, so they tried to copy that person. One person told me he was going to pray two hours each day because he read in a book about someone who did. He later told me, "I fell asleep after twenty minutes." It is not the length of our prayers that's as important as the quality of them.

Peter once prayed, *"Lord, save me"* when he tried to walk on water as Jesus was doing. Just a three-letter prayer and it was answered. One of the two thieves who died on the cross next to Jesus cried, *"Lord, remember me when You come into Your kingdom,"* and his prayer was wonderfully answered.

God hears us not because our prayer is good, but because God is good. —A.W. Tozer

Here are some prayer helps not just for beginners, but for anyone who struggles to have a consistent life of prayer. These suggestions are taken first from my study of prayer in the Bible, and from my own experience.

1. WHEN IS THE BEST TIME TO PRAY?

Anytime is the best. I'm a morning person, but I didn't used to be. My brother David Wilkerson known for his prayer life always prayed late in the evening. Psalm 55:17 says, *"Evening and morning and at noon, I will pray, and cry aloud."* This was written by David the Psalmist at a special time of trouble in his life. Exactly what it was we do not know, but reading the entire 55th Psalm, David speaks of *"terror befalling me"* (vs. 4) and he refers to being betrayed by a friend (vss. 12-14).

When we go through extraordinary times of difficulty, we can throw out all the normal guidelines on prayer. 911 calls are made based on the emergency. I have read that 911 prayers are criticized, but like Peter when he was about to sink and drown, any kind and any time prayers are needed in desperate cases.

A.W. Tozer, a prolific writer especially on prayer, prayed at various times in the furnace room of the basement of his home. Time and place vary with different people.

2. WHEN BEGINNING A TIME OF PRAYER, START WITH PRAISE AND THANKSGIVING.

If you went to a friend to help you with a need or problem, would you start the conversation right away, asking for help before even greeting him or her? Prayer is based on friendship, as in the natural so in the spiritual realm.

Psalm 104:4 says, *"Enter His gates with thanksgiving, and into His courts with praise: be thankful unto Him and bless His name."* A court is a place of authority. When we pray, especially in Jesus' name, He is our Advocate to take our prayers to the Father (1 John 2:1). It is not the force, frequency, and choice of words we use in prayer by which God hear us. It is Who we are praying to, and not how we pray. God hears our prayers, not because we're good at praying, but because He is good.

3. PRAY THE SCRIPTURES.

Someone told me that they would run out of things to say when praying. For me, that was hard to understand. I never have a hard time talking to my wife unless I know I've done something wrong and am in trouble with her.

I find a way to aid my prayer time is on occasion to pray the Psalms. Some of these Psalms have verses that may apply to you as you pray them, and some will not. Here are a few examples:

Psalm 31 (A few verses sample phrases)

- *"In You, O Lord, I put my trust...* (vs. 1)
- *"Bow down Your ear to me...* (vs. 2)
- *"Make your face to shine [on me]...* (vs. 16)

The Psalms are full of great prayers. Try reading these Scriptures as prayer to God. Obviously, you need to keep your eyes open (smile) when doing so. I often pray while driving. There is nothing in Scripture that says we ought to close our eyes when we pray.

4. IN PREPARATION FOR PRAYER, AT TIMES, LISTEN TO GOSPEL MUSIC.

As prayer brings to us things to which beget gratitude and thanksgiving, so praise and gratitude promote prayer, and induce more and better praying. —E.M. Bounds[30]

For me at times I like to listen to hymns or songs that set the atmosphere for prayer, especially songs of praise and thanksgiving. For example, I grew up in a church where we often sang, *"I need Thee, every hour, most gracious Lord. Come bless me now, my Savior. I come to Thee."* I like to find that on YouTube and listen to it during my devotional time. Another song good for prayer time is simply entitled, *"Praise the name of Jesus. He's my Rock, He's my Fortress, in Him will I trust."*

Pick out your favorite worship music that can invite the presence of the Lord and stimulate a time of prayer. When I worship God, it's like a canopy covers me and I feel absolutely shut in with the Lord. It's impossible for the unbeliever to worship. Prayer and worship are the twin blessings for believers to experience.

As I was writing this, I woke up and did not have my usual morning prayer because I had to hurry off to an appointment. It was a thirty-minute drive to the appointment, so I turned on my Satellite Radio to a gospel music station and as I drove, I had a great time of prayer and praise, keeping my eyes open!

5. IT'S OKAY TO MISS
YOUR USUAL PRAYER TIME.

I know what's it like when travelling long distances to miss my daily prayer time. I don't condemn myself for this. Christians should not be like devout Muslims who have daily prayer as a ritual. In their case, prayer is just a routine with connection with the Holy Spirit. It has no more meaning than when we might say hello to a neighbor.

Avoid turning prayer into a legalistic practice. If you do, it can lose its meaning, sort of when someone nonchalantly makes the sign of the cross. It's a good thing to do, but it can be more a habit than anything else.

This prayer guideline is not for those who don't have a prayer time ever. If that's you, start a daily habit of prayer and keep it up within the context of your everyday life; and if occasionally you miss a prayer time, there are ways to make it up as I will share in the next point.

6. TAKE A PRAYER BREAK INSTEAD OF A COFFEE BREAK.

There are students who take prayer breaks, moments for silent prayer in school. In like manner, one can do the same sitting at a desk in an office having silent prayer or even while drinking coffee, lifting thoughtful prayers between sips. Prayer is something that takes us into the supernaturally naturally. After all, Jesus instituted the sacred act of communion around a supper table.

Those who desire to pray will always find a time and a place to pray. One woman used dish washing time to pray. Another used her ironing time to pray. I watched with amazement as NFL football players from both teams knelt for prayer before a game. Tim Tebow, a college football star, was shown numerous times after scoring a touchdown in the end zone knelling and praying. I have witnessed many times professional athletes, primarily NFL football players, doing the same. One field goal kicker always makes the sign of the cross before he kicks the ball.

The closest the average person can pray privately yet in a way publicly is before eating in a restaurant. Nowadays, it's rare to see, but occasionally I do witness this. My wife and I observed a mother and her adult daughter praying in a booth across from us. We finished eating before they did and when we left I passed their table and leaned over and said, "Thank you for praying before your meal." They both smiled!

Coffee breaks, mealtimes, and work time pauses are opportunities to pray, either silently or softly — and it's a good witness to others.

7. GOD HEARS SILENT PRAYER!

Thought prayer are heard as much as voiced prayers, especially when in a place or situation where if your prayed aloud they might call EMS workers to come and take you away. When I can't sleep, which at my age happens more often than not, I lie awake, but my mind is active in prayer. It's not unusual for the Holy Spirit as such times to bring to mind a person I had not thought about, even for years, and I have a burden to pray for them.

I went alone into our chapel at Brooklyn Teen Challenge one day for some personal prayer. The burden of helping addicts, especially financially, in a faith-funded program was almost always a weight I carried. As I was praying softly and silently, someone came and knelt also at the altar to my left. I knew it was someone who'd just come in off the streets and entered our program. I knew this without looking up because of the fresh smell of the streets oozing from his clothes and body. He began to pray a simple prayer. I don't recall the exact words, but it was something like, "God, please help me. Please change me." At that moment, I was overcome with the difference between me and him. We both mainly were praying silent prayers. What blessed me is that in the contrast between myself and this street addict, I might have thought I had more of a right for God to hear my prayer. But that pray-er next to me had as much right for God to answer his prayer as mine. His was a simple and mostly silent sinner's prayer.

After the disciples had argued as to who would be greatest in God's future kingdom, it says in Luke 9:47, "*And Jesus perceived the thought of their heart.*" If our less than godly thoughts are known, how much more our holy ones. Psalm 139:1-2 says, "*Oh Lord, you have searched me and know me. You know my sitting down and my rising up; you understand my thoughts afar off.*" If God perceived the carnal thoughts of His disciples, how much more will He know our thoughts and silent prayers.

One of the points of this is that we can think prayer is primarily what happens in church or at scheduled times. James 4:8 says, "*Draw near to God and He will draw near to you.*" Drawing near to God anytime and anywhere is appropriate.

8. PRAY FOR THE UNSAVED!

Of course, we should pray privately for the unsaved, especially for unsaved family members, loved ones, and friends. However, one of perhaps the least used kind of prayers is one not used in evangelism.

Recently, I was on the streets of an inner city that was full of drug addicts. I approached a young man that was reeling like a zombie, very high on drugs. I asked him if I could pray for him? He said, "No, thanks," so I honored that. What I should have done was to step aside and pray silently for him. We should be careful when witnessing to others to not be too aggressive in our witness, including if they do not want prayer. However, a lost opportunity can be in not asking to pray for them, or not stopping to pray for them privately if they refuse our offer.

My mother, now with the Lord, was sort of a street preacher and pray-er. She was not one to stand on a street corner and share the gospel. But she would engage people in conversation in a motherly way. Almost always she'd ask, "May I pray for you?" If the person hesitated, she took that for a yes and would begin to pray for them. What she and I learned from that is when you pray for someone, they recognize it as a sacred moment. Prayer brings the presence of God, and even if the unsaved person does not recognize it, God does, and the person knows in some kind of way something they can't define is taking place.

9
LESSONS FROM MY PRAYER STORIES

In my preaching and teaching ministry, I often tell stories. They usually are personal in nature that hopefully are relevant to the truths I seek to convey. These lessons are on faith, hope, change, deliverance, and prayer. I will conclude this book with selected prayer stories from growing up in a family where personal and family prayer was a daily practice. I also include testimonies—stories from some 65 years of working with drug addicts, alcoholics, and others with various life-controlling problems. I led a ministry in which Bible-based teaching and counseling (together with praise, worship, and prayer) was an integral part of the program. Each story has a title corresponding to the lesson I share.

EXAMPLE 1
"No, thank you. I got my own stuff."
TONY AND THE DRUG PUSHER

Tony was four months in the Lord. He asked for a pass home to celebrate his mother's birthday (at least that's what he claimed). He was from Spanish Harlem in Manhattan, New York, the very area where he had attended one of our open-air street rallies and accepted Christ. That same night he did, we enrolled him into our program. He had a true Jesus encounter.

When he asked for an unaccompanied home visit, I thought, "Do I have faith in him and faith the gospel of Christ to keep him from temptation?" I granted him permission for a home visit. But first, he went into the chapel and had a short time of prayer.

Some hours later, he returned with this testimony after bursting in the door all excited. He said, "Pastor, I now know I'm free."

He explained that, as he rode the subway to Harlem, he kept silently praying, "Jesus, keep me strong. Please, Jesus." When he got to his street and was walking towards his apartment, he noted that none of his friends were there; none of the prostitutes either, or no drug pushers. He went inside the apartment and prayed a prayer of thanksgiving: *"Lord, thank You for clearing the streets for me."*

After several hours, it was time to head to the mean streets again and back to Brooklyn, hopefully without incident. As he walked to the subway, he looked around again and still the streets were clear of what he considered danger.

But then! Seemingly out of nowhere, he heard a voice: "Hey, Tony! You lookin' good. Where you been?" The voice had a face to it that Tony knew well. A drug connection. The seller assumed, because Tony had put on some weight, he had either just been in detox or in jail. He said to Tony, "I got some stuff! You need?"

Tony momentarily froze.

For the sake of this lesson, let me put this in terms of the point of this story: The moment fear stared Tony in the face is called temptation. In Tony's case, this was a temptation by which he could have destroyed sixteen weeks of sobriety and victory!

Now, as a reader, you may have been in the same place as Tony. His temptation represents the "stuff" the devil dangles before our eyes. How will you face it? Here's how Tony reacted.

When the pushed said, "Tony you want stuff?" meaning heroin. He simply said, "No, thank you. I got my own stuff." Of which the pusher said, "Where are you connecting now?"

Tony said, "Brooklyn! I found a new connection. His name is Jesus," and proceeded to share his Christ-centered testimony. His friend, now a former friend, just walked away, mumbling, "Man, you're crazy. You won't last long. I'll be here when you come back. I've never seen anyone escape this hellhole."

This then was Tony's victory story as he shared with me on his successful return.

THE LESSONS

1. Pray this prayer before the fact, rather than after the mess up.

Watch and pray, lest you enter into temptation. The spirit is willing, but the flesh is weak (Matthew 26:41).

Prayer gives you spiritual muscle to withstand temptation.

2. **Stand on this promise, whether like Tony you're new in the Lord, or you've been walking with the Lord for some time:**

No temptation has overtaken you except as is common to man; but God is faithful, who will not allow you to be tempted beyond what you are able, but with the temptation will also make the way of escape, that you make be able to bear it (1 Corinthians 10:13).

EXAMPLE 2
"DAVIE, YOU'RE NOT THE ONLY ONE WHO CAN PRAY."

In the ministry of Teen Challenge that my brother David Wilkerson founded, I'm considered co-founder with him. The first street gang leader who accepted Christ was Nicky Cruz of the Mau-Mau gang of Fort Greene, Brooklyn. There was no residential rehab center/home at the time. So, my brother discipled Nicky by just keeping him with him as much as possible. This included taking Nicky with him to Phillipsburg, Pennsylvania where my brother was pastor before he moved to New York City to open a full-time ministry to gangs and soon afterwards to drug addicts.

Besides David home-discipling Nicky, he would take him with him when having speaking engagements. Once, on a trip to Chicago, they stayed in a hotel for several nights with each having their own adjacent room. During the afternoon and before the evening service, Nicky could hear my brother praying. The same was when he was in David and Gwen's home. At the time, Nicky just thought prayer was for pastors exclusively, something they were required to do as a part of their calling.

One day when they met in the morning Nicky said, "Davie (the name my brother was known for in the church and community where he was the pastor) you're not the only one who can pray." And so, prayer became a part of Nicky's discipleship early on in his walk with God.

THE LESSONS

1. Prayer is not for specially called people. It is, and should be, a practice adopted immediately after the experience of the new birth in Christ.

After the coming of the Holy Spirit on the day of Pentecost, *"Those who gladly received his word* [referring to Peter's gospel-message] *were baptized. And they continued steadfastly in the apostle's doctrine and fellowship, in the breaking of bread, and in prayers"* (Acts 2:40-42). Among them were Jesus' disciples. But they were not professionals, were not famous [as we today known them to be]. They were like their brothers and sisters in Christ and the newest convert knew prayer is what every believer does as a matter of daily habit.

God did not hear Martin Luther's or Billy Graham's prayers because they had a famous name, but because they prayed in Jesus' name! *"Whatever you ask in My name, that I will do, that the Father may be glorified in the Son"* (John 14:13). Note, it does not say whoever will ask in their name. The only name-dropping that counts in heaven is Jesus. *"Therefore God has also highly exalted Him and given Him a name which is above every name"* (Philippians 2:9).

2. Prayer does not make the one who prays regularly holy.

It should be as natural as breathing, quenching one's thirst, or eating daily meals. What makes the body strong is the daily intake of air, water, and food. Likewise, prayer is the outflow of conversations with God followed by the inflow of His Spirit. It also sets God to work in answer to our prayers. Beware of the Pharisaical prayer that Jesus warned about:

> And when you pray, you shall not be like the hypocrites. For they love to pray standing in the synagogues and on the corners of the streets, that they may be seen by men (Matthew 6:5).

Jesus spoke of the importance of private prayers, and they are the privilege of all classes, races, ages, social positions, the rich, the poor, the educated, and the uneducated, as long as these come from the heart before they pass through the lips.

EXAMPLE 3
"OH, JESUS, JESUS, JESUS...PLEASE HELP ME!"

The quote above is a part of the Kenneth and Ann Wilkerson's (my parents) family history. It's been carried down through the generations of myself and my siblings when the above cry of "Jesus, Jesus, Jesus, help" was uttered by our brother Jerry whenever he got in trouble and my father would take his belt in hand to give Jerry a good spanking. As far as I know, my brother cried that prayer only once and Jesus apparently answered his prayer, for on the occasion he hollered that prayer to Jesus, the whipping never happened.

Dad used to tell this story when we were grown and sharing family stories and secrets. Apparently, the manner of Jerry's desperately prayer caused my father to laugh so hard that he lost the desire to carry out the punishment. I would retell this story in sermons and teaching on pray, sharing the following lessons.

LESSONS

1. God hears our prayer when we're in trouble.

Psalm 55:22 (quoted in *The Message* a modern contemporary version) says, "Pile your troubles on God's shoulders—

he'll carry your load, he'll help you out.
He'll never let good people topple into
ruin."

It apparently does not matter whether we or
others are the cause of our trouble. He still invites us
to come to Him. I do believe when we cry out to God
when in trouble of our own making, the way He
answers will be different than if others or difficult
circumstances causes the trouble. In self-inflicted
troubles the Lord usually answers in a way that He
allows redemptive punishment to take place, so we
learn the needed lesson.

Here's a few promises when praying when in
trouble:

- May the Lord answer you in the day of trouble,
  may the name of the God of Jacob defend you
  (Psalm 20:1).

- I will be glad and rejoice in your mercy, for You
  considered my trouble" (Psalm 31:7).

2. God is neither nervous nor deaf to our prayers. Loud is okay; soft and natural are better.

When Jesus prayed for Lazarus to come forth
from the grave *"He cried with a loud voice, 'Lazarus come
forth'"* (John 11:43). It's been said the reason Jesus did
not just say *"Come forth"* is that all the dead would

have come out of the graves. We also learn from this to be specific in our prayers.

> When we are specific in our prayers, God can be specific in His answers. —David Wilkerson

3. When in trouble, prayers often come from a repentant heart.

I believe my brother Jerry's loud and specific cry to God was from a repentant heart. *"Man that is willing to repent will find God."* —A.W. Tozer[31] Jerry's cries to God were saying in effect, "Please help me. I know I did wrong." Knowing my brother as I did, I knew he had a tender heart towards God as evidenced by the fact he cried "Jesus" three times.

If our troubles are the result of our own sin and wrongdoing, then repentance is essential.

APPENDIX
SCRIPTURE PRAYERS FROM THE PSALMS

Donald S. Whitney wrote,

> Why the Psalms? God gave the Psalms to us so that we could give the Psalms back to God. No other book in the Bible was inspired for that express purpose. So, in the Psalms, God teaches us to come before Him using the following.[32]

PSALM 3:1 You, O Lord, are a shield about me.

PSALM 8:1 O Lord, our Lord, how majestic is your name in all the Earth! You have set your glory above the heavens.

PSALM 16:11 You make known to me the path of life; in Your presence, there is fullness of joy; at Your right hand, are pleasure forevermore.

PSALM 36:7 How precious is your steadfast, love, O God!

PSALM 51:17 A broken and contrite heart, O God, you will not despise.

PSALM 71:19 Your righteousness, O God, reaches the high heavens. You have done great things, O God, who is like You?

PSALM 77:13 Your way, O God, is holy, what god is great like our God?

PSALM 85:6 You, O Lord, are good and forgiving, abounding in steadfast, love to all who call upon You.

PSALM 104:1-2 Oh Lord, my God, you are very great! You are clothed with splendor and majesty, covering Yourself with light as a garment, stretching out to heaven like a tent.

PSALM 119:105 Your word is a lamp to my feet and I light to my path.

PSALM 139:1-2 O Lord, you have searched me and known me! You know when I sit down, and when I rise up; You discern my thoughts from afar.

(The above verses are from the ESV Bible/)

THE PRAYERS OF DAVID

(The following are from the NEW LIVING TRANSLATION)

PSALM 16:1-2 Keep me safe, O God, for I have come to you for refuge. I said to the Lord, "You are my Master! Every good thing I have comes from You."

PSALM 16:7-8 I will bless the Lord, who guides me; even at night, my heart instructs me. I know the Lord is always with me. I will not be shaken, for He is right beside me.

PSALM 18:1-5 I love you, Lord; You are my strength. The Lord is my rock, my fortress, and my savior; my God is my rock, and whom I find protection. He is my shield, the power that saves me, and my place is safety. I called on the Lord, who is worthy of praise, and he saved me from my enemies.

PSALM 23 The Lord is my shepherd; I have all I need. He lets me rest in green pastures; He leads me besides peaceful streams. He renews my strength. He guides me along right paths, bringing honor to His name. Even when I walk through the darkest valley, I will not be afraid, for You are close beside me. Your rod and Your staff protect and comfort me. You prepare a feast for me in the presence of my enemies. You order me by anointing my head with oil. My cup overflows with blessing. surely goodness and unfailing love will pursue me all the days of my life, and I will live in the house of the Lord forever.

PSALM 25:1-2, 4-5 O Lord, I give my life to You. I trust in You, my God! Do not let me be disgraced. Show me the right path, O Lord; point out the road for me to follow. Lead me by Your truth and teach me, for You are the God who saves me. All day long I put my hope in you.

PSALM 27:1-4 The Lord is my light and my salvation—So why should I be afraid? The Lord is my fortress, protecting me from danger. So why should I tremble? The one thing I seek of the Lord—the thing I seek most—is to live in the house of the Lord all the days of my life, delighting in the Lord's perfection and meditating in his temple.

PSALM 63:1-5 O God, you are my God, I earnestly search for You. My soul thirst for You, my whole body it longs for You in this parched and weary land where there is no water. I have seen You in your sanctuary and upon Your power and glory. Your unfailing love is better than life itself. How I praise You! I will praise You as long as I live, lifting up my hands to You in prayer. You satisfy me more than the richest feast. I will praise You with songs of joy. I lie awake thinking of you, meditating on you through the night. Because You are my helper, I sing for joy in the shadow of Your wings. I cling to you. Your strong right hand holds me securely.

ENDNOTES

[1] Tozer, A.W. *Prayer: Communing with God in Everything-Collected Insights from A.W. Tozer*. Moody Publishers. Kindle Edition.

[2] Spurgeon, Charles. *Spurgeon on the Priority of Prayer (Spurgeon Speaks)*. Moody Publishers. Kindle Edition.

[3] Nathan Markee. *I Can Pray*. Source Musixmatch, Ashville Music Publishing.

[4] Simpson, Charles. *The Bosom of the Father: The Place Jesus Has Prepared For Us*. Kindle Edition.

[5] Krummacher, Dr. F.W. *Daily Christian Quotes,* January 9, 2010. https://www.dailychristianquote.com/dr-f-w-krummacher/

[6] Babcock, Maltbie D. Lyrics to *This is My Father's World*. (1901) https://hymnary.org/text/this_is_my_fathers_world

[7] Tozer, A.W. *Delighting in God* (DF Christian Bestsellers). Digital Fire. Kindle Edition.

[8] Harsant, Andy. Lyrics to Heaven Came Down. Source Musixmatch, Ashville Music Publishing.

[9] A German proverb, Source Unknown.

[10] Grumm, William. Lyrics to *Shut in with God*. https://hymnary.org/hymn/IGSD1943/page/40

[11] Derricks, Cleavant. Lyrics to Just A Little Talk With Jesus. https://hymnary.org/text/i_once_was_lost_in_sin_but_jesus_took_me.

[12] Tozer, A.W. *Prayer: Communing with God in Everything-Collected Insights from A.W. Tozer*. Moody Publishers. Kindle Edition.

[13] Tozer, A.W. *Delighting in God* (DF Christian Bestsellers). Digital Fire. Kindle Edition.

[14] Crosby, Fanny. Lyrics to *Draw Me Nearer*. https://hymnary.org/text/i_am_thine_o_lord_i_have_heard_thy_voice

[15] Bounds, E.M. *The Necessity of Prayer.* Kindle Edition.

[16] Ibid.

[17] Ibid.

[18] Morgan, Reuben. Lyrics from *This Is My Desire.* Hillsong Music.

[19] Bounds, E.M. *The Necessity of Prayer.* Kindle Edition.

[20] Ibid.

[21] Tozer, A.W. *The Pursuit of God.* Moody Publishers. Kindle Edition.

[22] Dunlop, Merrill. Lyrics from *My Sins Are Blotted Out, I Know!* https://hymnary.org/text/what_a_wondrous_message_in_god s_word

[23] Wilkerson, Don. *The Challenge Study Bible.* Bridge-Logos Publishers.

[24] Carter, Russel Kelso. Lyrics from *Standing on the Promises.* https://hymnary.org/search?qu=Standing+on+the+Promises

[25] Ibid.

[26] Ibid.

[27] Wilkerson, Don. *29:11 The Jeremiah Code.* Bridge-Logos Publishers. Kindle Edition.

[28] Augustine, St. *The Confessions of St. Augustine.* Kindle Edition.

[29] *Chain Breaker.* Written by: Jonathan Lindley Smith, Mia Fieldes, Zach Williams. Lyrics © ESSENTIAL MUSIC PUBLISHING

[30] Bounds, E.M. *The Essentials of Prayer.* Kindle Edition.

[31] Tozer, A.W. *The Pursuit of God.* Moody Publishers. Kindle Edition.

[32] Whitney, Donald S. *Praying the Bible.* Crossway. Kindle Edition.

ACKNOWLEDGEMENTS

A thank you to Kristy Johnson for her good editing work on this manuscript.

An appreciation to Charles Simpson for his formatting of the manuscript in preparation for publication. In addition, I thank him for his encouragement in my various writing projects.

Please check out some of my other books at

Amazon.com.

(My most recent book is entitled
12 Step Through the Bible, A Bible-Based Version of the Traditional 12 Steps of A.A.)

**Your comments are welcomed.
You may contact me at:**

beholdm416@gmail.com

Made in the USA
Columbia, SC
22 October 2024

ed318705-0e61-4a83-aae4-f49e3a880ddeR01